3 | 13

DATE DUE FOR RETURN

Renewals
www.liverpool.gov.uk/libraries
0151 233 3000

Clavics

THE DAYBOOKS IV

CLAVICS

Geoffrey Hill

ENITHARMON PRESS

First published in 2011
by Enitharmon Press
26B Caversham Road
London NW5 2DU

www.enitharmon.co.uk

Distributed in the UK by
Central Books
99 Wallis Road
London E9 5LN

Distributed in the USA and Canada
by Dufour Editions Inc.
PO Box 7, Chester Springs
PA 19425, USA

ISBN: 978-1-907587-11-5 (regular edition)
ISBN: 978-1-907587-12-2 (signed limited edition)

Enitharmon Press gratefully acknowledges the financial support of
Arts Council England, London.

The drawing by Robert Webb on page 5, after a design by Inigo Jones for
Whitehall Palace, is reproduced from John Harris, Stephen Orgel and Roy Strong,
The King's Arcadia: Inigo Jones and the Stuart Court (London: Arts Council, 1973). The intaglio
engraving on page 45 is reproduced from the facsimile edition of Comenius's
Orbis Pictus (1659) published by Oxford University Press in 1968.

British Library Cataloguing-in-Publication Data.
A catalogue record for this book is available
from the British Library.

Typeset in Joanna
and printed in England by
Antony Rowe Ltd

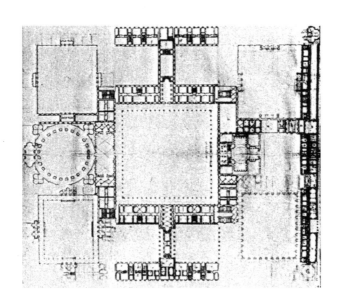

To Chris and Christine Woodhead

CLAVICS: The science or alchemy of keys — OED, 2012

Be very var vith his raklese toyis of Padoa

Ah! taci ingiusto core

1

Bring torch for Cabbalah brand new treatise,
Numerology also makes much sense,
    O *Astraea*!
    Watch us conform
    To the immense
    Lore, hypertense
    Attaching to the swarm-
    Ing mass, the dense
Fluctuations of the materia
Out from which I shall be lucky to twitch
    Creative fire.
    See where who goes?
    Astraea, bitch! —
    Protean ditch
    Suffices what she does
    Returning rich
To the low threshold of contemplation
Her servile master subsisting on scraps
    Keeping station
As one pursuing ethics perhaps.

Intensive prayer ís intensive care
    Herbert says. I take it stress marks
    Convey less care than flair
    Shewing the works
    As here
    But if
    Distressed attire
    Be mere affect of clef
    Dump my clavic books in the mire
And yes bid me strut myself off a cliff.

2

Torching Cabbalah not a fine refrain.
Set on the dais drudging Uccello's
Cruel *Profan-*
Ation that smug
Trim and callous
Custom allows
Best employ dialogue
Views before vows:
O I will give you your profanation
Cries the man with his back to the black stake
But a notion
That I am not
Here and awake
To spit and crack
Bonds my voice to my throat.
Dance jumping jack.
How did I so incline to this subject?
Because aesthetics are an inclined plane.
I would object
Mildly to seeing the object again.

Metaphysical intensifiers
Barely a paradox: they say
Inessential repairs
Would wouldn't they
Cracked squires
Built kites
Gave themselves airs
Setting the laws to rights,
Hazard's itinerants the stars.
Meritocrats are crap meteorites.

3

As good epitaphs go Will Lawes is slain
Permit me, sire, is slain by such whose wills
       Be laws. Again
       Swift and neat hand
       Notate the viols
       Flexures of styles
      Extravagant command
       Purposeful frills
What comes of the upthrust and downthrust pen
These fantasies constrained by their own strings
      Narcissus then
      Crowns fantasy
      Feasts what feast brings
      Imaginings
    Consort like winter sky
      Drawn from the wings.
Jolt into the epilogue by your leave
As into a mixed skirmish, a rout,
      Punched semibreve
Like fatal bullet through the fine slashed coat.

Because metaphysic is what you will
  Marking time is not bearing time
    As   inevitable
    The pale sun's rime
    Until
    No sun
    No dying climb
   Statute's oxymoron
  Impassionate lost thistle-rhomb
No intercept from zero friskly drawn.

4

Cultic beyond reason that king-martyr.
He was a double-dealer, betrayed friends
      Without quarter.
      Parliament
      Waved its black wands;
      The deodands
    Of sick spittle and cant
      Stained the altar.
The grace of music is its dissonance
Unresolved beneath resolution
      Of flow and stance:
      Our epic work –
      Cadenced nation –
      Figuration
      Running staidly amok,
      Discord made dance.
I am conspired, thinking best of our selves;
Chronic self-willing that with Furor feints;
      Justice devolves;
Conjures disjunction into printers' founts.

Take the old issue with chromatic tunes
  False relation, dishabitude
  Of polity, dead loans
    Anarchs beside
    Lost thrones
    A m e n d
    Our sovran maims
  Be to love as well-found
  Drive slow instauration of themes
Grant fidelity to heterophones

5

Making of mere brightness the air to tremble
So the sun's aurora in deep winter
Spiders' bramble
Blazing white floss
Silent stentor! –
Viscosity and dross
No more amass
At the centre
The whole anatomy of heaven and earth
Shewn as the alchemists declare it
Poised beyond wrath
Resurrection
Of skin and bone
To dispirit . . .
The day cuts a chill swath,
Dark hunkers down.
I think we are past Epiphany now.
Earth billows on, its everlasting
Shadow in tow
And we with it, fake shadows onward casting.

Trust you to be a comic poet manqué
Evidence too sweet to dismiss
See above. Well, *thank* you!
(Taking the piss,
Donkey?)
Confess
M e l a n c h o l y
A touch too much my thing.
E r a s m u s , *In Praise of Folly* :
Grand antidote no substitute for bling

6

The enabling reader, the recusant
At my fingertips, for whom I write well
    Into my scant-
    Extended age
    This ritual
    Taking its toll
    Much like the saxifrage
    Breaking a wall:
On her reciprocal being, regard
For decorum, I now dread to renege
    A further word
    So tenuous
    The catalogue
    Heroic blague
    Bequeaths us and our vows
    Ardour toward:
Her I embolden, wife to Mallarmé.
Together we shall enrich the cortège
    Pli selon pli
Mathematicall Roses yet the rage.

Could be an emblem of some consequence
    Without thinking. How to derive
    Virtue from ponce to prince –
    Virtù – and thrive
    By glance:
    B e l i e v e
    T h e   r h e t o r i c
    O r   n o t ;   a n y   a r c h i v e
    Will demonstrate a plethoric
Rigour of stock conservation you dunce

7

Our children stepping backward through the years
As wrong-footed warriors, prophetic
                Of all arrears
                Nineteen sixteen
                Caught in static
                So what appears
            Blindly upon the screen
                Ghosting vatic
Outlines of projects for which these obliged
Mostly declaring good will with dissent
                To the hate-phaged
                Futurists yet
                As backward bent
                On advancement,
            Their own enfuried rote?
                O wronged extant
And still forgotten souls of the slain
Bowed to be made memorable by lot
                The evergreen
Processionals tarnish held on remote.

Let them set aside ten minutes each way
    For public condolence, prayer
    By those who will not pray
        I n a y - s a y e r
            You say
            Well then
        H a u l   i r o n y
    Upon its rack; refrain
  Clavics archaic iron key:
Splash blessings on dead in Afghanistan.

8

How far give attestation its free ride –
A fair question. Poetry is eccentric
        Labour of pride;
        Fixates power;
        Fixes mantric
        Pitch and con trick;
     Nor hewer nor drawer;
        Not romantic.
Claim that it rises to its own jerked bait
Cites polity its *raison* among such
        Affairs of State
        You, I, might name,
        Set within touch
        Of heightened speech
    In some awed interim.
        You believe that?
I remit your citations, Lord Apollo,
Bestower of conundrums. Try me: what
        Flex to allow
Fixing this swing-arm with its counterweight.

Listen to and make music while you can
    Pray *Mater ora Filium*
      Cry *Spem in Alium*
        God is made man
        Choric
         Lyric
       Heaven receives
      Impartial these tributes
    Creation call it that believes
Even to blasphemy in our ranged throats.

9

Edgy, you say, cagy, strange edginess.
Check the electric circuits, you booby.
> Brushes a mess;
> Check them again;
> A fine hobby!
> Feeling clubby
> Largely eases the pain.
> Perish nobly.
Should benefit from this mixed blood and flame
Utterance known first to the haruspex
> And then to fame.
> Best are logged on
> By paradox
> As with drab sex
> By desire to have done
> Old meretrix.
Mystic emendation shall be called for;
Metaphysical intensifiers
> Well enrolled-for.
Not all the bad poets are bad liars.

Revealed thus as a type of figured bass
> Enriched ad libitum by hand
> Of cute accompanist:
> Hear the quills click
> *My son*
> *My son*
> The strings are slack
> Will Lawes *is broke* at Chest-
> Er; Lycidas lies in the sand;
Both justified. England rides rich on loss.

10

Intuitive mathematics' reason —
Be so of that Grace and bleed into it:
  This phosphor-fruit
  Void of season
  Re-examine
 Lumen de Lumine
  I intuit
  That you do not.
By this much I mean only mystical
And eccentric, though with centrist leanings.
  Sophistical
  Is in part truth
  Where part is all-
  Overing foil:
 Registered azimuth
  With trade shinings.
Would I were pardoned the effluent virus
Pardoned that sick program of pregnant odes.
  Near admirers
Cope with our begging Nescafé and rides.

You who have edited Ben Jonson's masques —
 All credit to your endeavours.
  (Coelum Britannicum
  Is not Jonson's)
  That said
  He had
  Many mansions
 Each with many a room;
 Majesty's divine cadavers
Poised as presiding deities sans tusks.

11

Plug in a dissonance to make them wince.
Density a workable element.
Name-acclaim once –
Reclaimed ransom
Truth from figment
Picks its fragment.
Somewhere such a kingdom
Roughed assonance.
Judith of Bethulia's well wrested
Calm. How controverted we have become,
Questor quested;
Answerable;
Outside the frame
You can't draw from
Old dense pin-stabbed Bible
Unmolested.
Somewhere is sacramental belonging.
Here we find but banking with God's grammar
Strung unstringing
Grace from chance, worked like a novice stammer.

Democracy is a Potemkin fiction
Anarchical Plutocracy
Proliferates its gyre
Photo-couvade:
How could
you? said
Savage, like glad.
More substance than we are?
Phantom-chasing Natocracy.
Richard Dadd dab-hand at prize depiction.

12

Between dissatisfaction and finish
Is where it goes wrong. Getting under way
    The things vanish
    Marvellously;
    Leave as coda
    Some form of code
   Like sonnets of Spanish
    Autocracy.
Yes, I heard her: *my self-abnegation*
And drug-taking. I am in my right mind
    Do you still find?
    So that I spell
    And keep station?
    Arrogation
   Of entitled travail
    Contempt of kind.
Ah, but the wound of love is never healed!
While male and female voices busk and thrill
    The air grows riled:
Insidious the epiphanic spill.

As you were, exiting philosopher;
   Anything numen of desire
    And neurocratic hope.
    Pass angel. Drop
    Azured
    Lizard.
    Closed inquiries
   Open to chimaeras
   And other energies: attained
Absolute relativity of mind.

13

Don't accost me here on anomalies —
Will Lawes auditioning for Ronnie Scott,
      Alto sax, lute —
      So he survives
      Demi-famous
      The rakish hat
    Musicianship that moves
      Oddly in state.
Why do you so plug *wit and drollery?*
Clop-clip-clop, ups with his troop to Chester
      Unmerrily
      To register,
      To be felled, *slain*,
      Etcetera;
    In what corpse-rift unknown;
      Riffraffed the day.
Lawes makes his way in grinding the textures
Of harmony; so I think, here's a mind
      Would have vexed yours
With late unharpied bounty wrought to find.

What else here fit but mimicked *consort setts*
  Patterns that crown elaborate
    True deliberation
    Fantasies come
      At cost:
      At best
    In crossing rhyme
  Shake a crosspatched nation.
  Small chance factoring at such rate
Wrote finish to, not stasis of, regrets.

14

Concurring that the old man is in shock
Won't do; the shocked are rarely so brazen.
          Timed by Great Clock
          Lyric-loutish
          Plays of swineherds
          And severed heads;
          Buzzle of things loutish
          And things weazen;
Verses metronome-safe to emote by;
Tuning to spirit voices for control.
          Nightmare of school:
          There stands the Greek
          Hypotenuse
          With its long nose,
          Ruminating in black,
          Moved remotely.
Guide, pray, the mentally disadvantaged
Safe to Urbino; Yeats and your author
          Photomontaged,
Graciously inclined each to the other.

Bring out the leaden cope each hypocrite
          Dante makes wear: convoluted
          Sentence go hang. Marceau
          Mimed himself stuck;
          The last
          Mask-twist
          Paste face a-lock
          Fatalism of farce.
Give you first go, hell-rerouted
Light entertainers weighed with leaden wit.

15

Working divisions on a shift of line
Take it as a ground some worth debating
      Collocating
     As you find them
     Things to outshine
     Gold from the Rhine;
      May fortune attend them
      Scant words of mine.
Thus I foretold the grand Staffordshire hoard
Long since, without benefit of crystal,
      Went dazed, unread.
      Hullo, thistle,
      Silver-silk head,
      Gashed green-blue woad,
     Buoyant in old fallow,
      Watch by your dead.
Thus to relatinate Cranmer's commons,
Media vita − singing rings hollow −
      Still the summons:
We shall go down to bed with worm pillow.

Some super-charade of spirits and ghosts
  I heard the man say. Nabokov,
    To recall the topic.
     Dutifully
      It seems
      The screams
     Of butterfly,
  Moth, float through biopic
From his father's stretched mouth. *Book of*
Changes: outré silencings make ripostes.

16

Iniquitous heart, submit no new plea
As if to retell mere nonsense incurred;
  Logorrhea,
  Venus' lard,
  The singer's mouth
  Emetic-scarred;
 Travestied love, botched youth;
  Patrocleia
It is the lying in wait that demeans
Sanity of mind; even the sane thought
  Distrait, distraught;
  Purposed victim.
  One's best assigns
  Hector Troy's plains.
  How to depict you – them –
  Achilles' tort.
Bear with defoliate terrain, betray
Why one word follows another or how
  Your words toss prey
To their own orchidlike emollient jaw.

I'll beat you down – on sentiment as well –
 Ah, taci ingiusto core,
  Heart of all opera
  Rising sing swell
  To home
  On fame
  To aggrandize,
 Ingrate, veritable
Core, thy pulsings irritable
Gifts grantable yet out of hand mere prize.

17

Music cannot forever exhaust time.
Tell me what it is I labour around,
If you have found –
Chill me on style –
Rhyming *Coelum*
Britannicum
Such riches to entail,
Poenia crown'd
Through which her haire starts up like a furie.
Do not in any case mock invention
That holds story
To what it is:
By contention
Slight poetry
Pitching inquietus
To Usury.
Conclude: to wit, such lyric enrostered
With stage convention, swags and curlicues,
Word unbested,
Enriched out of Britannia her woes.

Opera enjoys the nefarious
As if innocently sublime
Ingiusto core. Try
Supplication
Of throes,
One does,
Confrontation
Without oratory,
Ah, taci, taci! In the womb
I could perform some of these arias.

18

Da capo — to give fantasy its head.
The eyes embrace us, *gravi e tardi*;
    A threnody
    Escapes the lips
    Moved in study.
    I have admired
    Dawkins's mortal quips
    As was required.
Straw men in flagrante folk-upbraided.
The champagne of St Pancras flows recured.
    Truth is austere
    I do believe.
    No deception
    Proved by caption,
    There is none to deceive . . .
    O the entire
Universe of Fun has begun to run
Down. While the Goodwin Committee en fête
    Is to debate
To some acid cud the taste of ruin.

Taci, ingiusto core! Not a hope.
    What is arrayed here sits engrained —
    No chip for excision —
    Such fine texture
    Of rage.
    Assuage
    Nothing. Text ire
    To a few whose mission —
    Here inadequately maligned —
Prays for redemption of your horoscope.

19

Into life we fell by brute eviction:
What prize brutish joy; what price compunction?
        To feel by trust
        Most things ill-won,
        Ill-held; even
        Your perfection
      Gross in its mistiming.
       In the dead mist
The fleet sweeps past, *Invincible*, others,
Derfflinger, *Grosser Kurfürst*; it is a dream
        Of undreaming,
        Chaste, all weathers.
        The journal ends
        Here in its fronds;
      Oblivious the calm
        Jolt of a wave.
That is an odd world from which to derive.
You may call ecrased a deep-whelmed acclaim.
        Forgo blaming
On the loss of Empire the spent compère.

You look at the thing; you think, *Not today.*
   Inopportunist Mechanics
     Adjust it otherwise
       Write as on slate.
        Yet I'd
        Concede
       Sensing the bite
     From the deep-laden rise
    Of the word my thrill; as sonics
Are to spheres where surely strange gods deploy.

.

20

Why I would not submit to young Rimbaud
Is beyond me: he is the Alchemist
   Taking to heart,
   The Supremo.
   It is so. Sic.
   Sex-alchemic.
  E R O T O M A N I A
   Drops people hurt.
Are you conning me simple rhyme? I am,
Bro. Ease this screw of paper from my fist.
   Give me your name
   So that I may
   Change. This drama
  Contrives well to persist,
   Some could deny.
   Take it away,
Your Grace, that folly be made a weird dream
Of salutation if not salvation,
   Constatation
Of the Cross I woke myself falling from.

Side-on spread wings, upright an hour-glass
  Better if egg-timer; barely
  A minute either way.
   This is our loss.
   Charles's
   Fane tolls
  I n d e c o r o u s
  Flesh restless to obey –
 Herbert times and twists text hereby:
Balanced glass wit let-tipple into Grace.

21

May be spared *The Dolphin?* Lost Book of Hours
This most tender of Presentations bears:
What the Lover's
Burden proffers
A cradled gift
The hard to lift
Soul of exacted Christ;
His almagest.
Intercept: why should all not be of some
Praeterient holding? Not too abrupt-
Ly break for home.
Unrest; at least
No narcolept,
I go in fear
Of Death's greed for the breast.
Is this so far
Departed New Age as to resuggest
Imbecility's fit raiment? But one
Candle lit on
The well-iced birthday slab so be my guest.

Worst of our age: no time here for patience
While there is a grand unwisdom
Legislates stun-wisdom
Buy quittance
Absurd
Last word
Stamped pittance
Although BAD LUCK! quizzdom
Scores well enough if you buzz bomb
Some sorry target aim pox Christians

22

What constitutes Metaphysics: you are
A revived soul like the spirit of Donne?
Or none; or none
Too bright a light.
Yet you rally.
I thought you might.
Sadly and hopefully
Climb to our sight-
Zenith, broad Jupiter. Not to desire
Sentiment on such track is difficult.
My fault my fault.
Sense the next line
Strike to result
From the dull melt.
Eager and unbenign
The click, the cult.
Will it be like leaving tokens to hand:
Tapes, I mean, unburned CDs, chinograph
Pencils; enough
Funky confessions funk-wise not to send?

I detect something false in that disquiet;
So let's mark time as it remains.
Fiction may find itself
Compatible
With truth
Like Ruth
In the Bible;
In a bright major clef;
Sul ponte, bearing on the strains;
Break C minor to C major at LIGHT.

23

Dearly beloved, grasp these sureties:
Decrepit lies the world and all things fail,
Exact their toll;
The Judgement must
Make trial, trust
Late Dorothy's —
Doctor D. Bethurum's —
Lorn expertise
Locked in her *Sermo Lupi ad Anglos*.
Give the old lady her due, concurreth
Doctor Pangloss.
We shall have sums
Right hand and left.
Lovely the Dooms,
These flaky; those bereft
Franciscan hymns:
Why then did you not call me in the night
To click the christian latch else dying might
With exequies
Of troubled phoenix ashes flame too bright?

New opinion on the rates of stall
Not forestalling major profits
All hands to the lever
C a l c u l a t i o n
Too right
Of fraught
A n i m a t i o n
Well endowed however
May overhear Minor Prophets
Cry that the Mercy of Things is not well

24

Alternative chronicity for this
Means our being the one flesh as flesh dies.
How this may have
Told us to grieve,
Mourn much as dread:
The Enigma's
Refusal to be read
By common eyes.
Alchemical desires: stars and stones,
Compassioning embraces – what disturbs,
Proliferates:
Poor recompense,
More nouns than verbs,
Some essence that dictates
How much defines
The end of sense.
Smudge-typed Admiralty communiqué
Pronouncing valediction: in dense skeins
Of frozen spray
Corvettes upwhelming through Icelandic day.

Touché – Archie Rice it should be but I've
Seen neither play nor film. Permit
Me stock adaptation
Of tradition
To touch
Was pitch;
Pre-coition
Secretly off ration.
Here you have me near as dammit
A *living voice* dead ringer for alive.

25

Very well, you shall redirect the pain —
May already have worked this — towards paean.
>Nothing bereaves
>Precisely; yet
>Lost springs of loves
>Turn things about
>>Upon the stiff axis
>Geared by bow staves;
Or as your indeterminate thriller —
Cannot relive even where it was put
>Down, in praxis,
>So misretrieves —
>This axle-tree,
>Mechanic root:
>Name fame one killer
>Propriety.
Ira quidem prodest quia corda
Reformat amantum: macaronic
>Thrills mute clinic —
Deaf child wailing into deaf ears, *sordo!*

Felicitas to conceive happiness,
>To have been where we met our eyes,
>But aware of gender,
>>Nor asunder:
>>Shew fouls
>>From those
>Bloody towels
>As bat-like embryos.
I have plumbed too much here to re-render.
Scrub yourself down from late-lamented guys.

26

Unity of knowledge — consilience —
The phrasing cribbed for I have no Science:
      Here infinite
      Clavics make spin,
      Keyed-in, commote,
     Tune the bees' element
      Compassed by scent-
      Colours and sun.
As to the ant when chance disturbs the State,
Divisions huge, minute, crude, delicate,
      Like egg-and-spoon
      White grub — rice grain —
      She works her reach
      With pitch and stretch,
     Staithed in that giant crèche.
      No metaphor.
The butterflies, high flyers on high winds;
Invisible to us they plane and soar
      Beyond our minds'
Troubled conventioning and do not err.

Stood with their martyr-king at Rowton Heath
   The Vaughan twins? Mêléeing big
    Scrap. Bonny there, Will Lawes
     Barneyed his death.
      No way
      Au fait
     How your rutter-
    Kin dabbles in these tacky shows.
  It must have been like sticking pig.
Talk of closure keeps open the matter.

27

Though they would warn me against world's regret,
The Vaughan brothers, Lawes presumably,
     Calculable
     As I confess
     Bulk of my fears;
     Theirs maybe not:
    World in its rot; but Faith
     Their good habit.
Gravitation something on which to click,
The Philosopher's Stone or Lotto luck;
     Absence of sloth,
     Irrelevant
     Virtue, discount.
    Virtù in sacred earth,
     Saint's bone. It may
     Be alchemy;
Though not all who treadle are gold-spinners.
Tom Vaughan an alchemist of the Cross
     Would price earth-dross
Mere tax on an infinitude of Sins.

. Shadows long wintering beneath the flare —
    Welsh once told kinship back to ninth
     Degree, much less so now —
     Declare Luna's
     Power:
     Thrawer
    Of benisons
   Benisons may bestow,
  Stilly riding her obscured plinth
Supremely unresponsive but aware.

28

In place of percentage absolution
Proclaim as best-tried ark for the nation
  Come Ash-Wednesday
  Corpus Christi
  When the bands play
  Smoke-hung feisty
  Catholic Lancashire
  Cry *ah my dear!*
For the likes of Tom Navvies and Poor Clares
Doctrine of the Immaculate Concept
  Read back transcript
  Of earth's desires
  Felix Randal
  Folk from Pendle
  That woman with the slop
  Pail on the step
Wrath and wrathful compassion so Dante
Stuck in the Epistle to Can Grande
  Virtues by will
Without them let us call plunder Plenty.

In strife of certitudes to be outstared.
Let me urge for myself virtues
Of the skald as hit-man
Things narrow thus
Chaos
Or chess
To harrow us
Go swanning through skidpan
As a freelance virtuoso
Other means of advancement undeclared

29

To speak of woe that is in marriage — Cal
Lowell after the Wife of Bath. Last chance.
Let out the cat
My bride my braut!
The cosmos-dance
Medieval
Touched up inheritance
Much to my heart.
Measured inconstancies of blood-sugars
Less unlikely than contests with cougars
In Clitheroe —
To speak of woe
And daemonry.
For harmony
Seek harmony in my
Unfeeling toe.
Always desire a homing, an epode;
Ask why you slaved for Otherness; be mad
Finally; wise
In default of difficult wisdom; God.

Calling to witness here the Winter Queen
The text wavers for cogency
On that remote screen
See, she is vexed.
Wotton
Spot on
In his context:
All lyric cries demean
Intricacy and urgency
The clouds not clouds of witness nor of scene.

30

Even less able to approach or end.
Things stood thus last time. So try periods.
But don't go there.
Merrier duds
Transmitted blind
Tortoise and hare
Divisions to the wire.
Tune out my mind
Speaks well of sensuous apprehension
Somebody in a different domain
Or dimension.
Segmental Man
Modulating
Take the *Rach Three*:
That will play your manhood
My young maestro!
I may be monstrously understating –
ETERNITY IRRADIATES COUPLE.
With none to care
Blank Cretaceous settled down this bubble.

Set yourself as finality avails
Conjurated ex-syllables
Tell most without saying
Configurate
Assign
Some coign
Of self-debate
Introvert surveying.
From blood-clay build what ennobles.
Untenable still the timeless values.

31

Haul in circumstantial intelligence
As Thomists handle nous; still so moving.
Radio-stars
Rake to find sense,
Truck with immense
Particulars.
Make no-one's disproving
Void evidence.
Right at the tether's end right to be free
Your centre ev'rywhere I cannot be:
Fully constrained
By hope, this lost
Freedom of mind-
Territory.
Ease to my foul bargains;
Grief and the rest.
Absolute for rage hold rage compliant
As Yeats, in his crazy-final refrains,
Bowed defiant.
A sunny window-sill and a stone plant.

Parasites essential to survivals.
Such teaching I have well absorbed
Long harbouring with grin
My enemy.
He talks
Well – Dawks –
Casts bonhomie
To all save Mortal Sin –
Root-proclivity and morbid –
Parasites intolerant of rivals.

32

There is a noise in my head: the breaking
Of sequence. Have worked to repletion
   Not yet disgust.
   As ever cost-
   Estimates fall
   Short of cost. Still,
  Before sleep, on waking,
   Know the eyes bleed.
Undertaken for honouring the dead
From our nation. Fulfilled in a thrusting
   Forward of rhyme
   Upon a theme
   Long protesting
   Some lame notion
  I had and have: barely
   But entirely
Devoted to those I disregarded,
Who looked to me, then; and no more retain
   The common pain.
From gapped inscripts let them gape recorded.

Trespass and consequence; misrequital;
 Lightly hidden lies equity.
  I shall not reveal how
   Much warmth was spent
   In ice
   Device.
  Is it slight cant
  Wishing to end well? Now
 Good occasion not to pity
Those so barely moved by such recital.

Clauſula.

The Cloſe.

Clavics has been typeset in Eric Gill's Joanna
and printed on 120gsm Munken Lynx Rough
in a regular edition of fifteen hundred copies.

The *de luxe* edition, bound and slipcased by
The Fine Book Bindery in Dubletta cloth
with Fabriano Tiziano endpapers,
consists of one hundred copies
signed and numbered 1/100 to 100/100
and twenty-five *hors commerce* copies
signed and numbered i/xxv to xxv/xxv.